Beginning at the star, cross out the first letter and every other letter in the grid. Then, write the remaining letters, in order, to solve the riddle.

★→ m	c	t	o
→ b	m	e	e
→ w	t	s	b
→ m	o	n	o
→ f	k	k	s

What do planets like to read?

___ ___ ___ ___ ___

___ ___ ___ ___ ___ !

Circle the word that is shown only one time in each box. Write the circled words, in order, to solve the riddle.

That	They
Then	
That	Then

bath	bath
both	
path	path

her	him
her	
have	him

part	park
park	
part	bark

How are trees and dogs alike?

_____ _____ _____ _____!

Write the correct vowel to finish each word. Use the clues to complete the crossword puzzle.

Across

2. 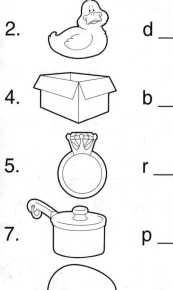 d ___ ck

4. b ___ x

5. r ___ ng

7. p ___ t

8.  ___ gg

Down

1. ___ x

3. c ___ r

4. b ___ g

6. n ___ t

7. 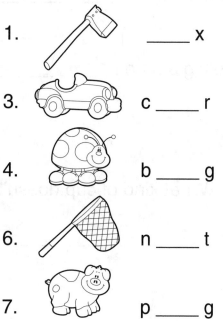 p ___ g

Unscramble each food word and write it on the lines. Then, write the circled letters, in order, to solve the riddle.

ohccoltea ___ ___ (___) ___ ___ ___ ___ ___

nsudae ___ (___) ___ ___ ___ ___

zzpia (___) ___ ___ ___ ___

rnppoco ___ ___ ___ (___) ___ ___ ___

ghspaetit ___ ___ (___) ___ ___ ___ ___ ___

ecnpaka ___ ___ ___ ___ (___) ___

mbugahrer ___ ___ ___ ___ ___ ___ (___) ___

What kind of cup doesn't hold water?

a ___ ___ ___ ___ ___ ___ ___

Use the secret code to solve the riddle.

How is food served on the moon?

___ ___
11   9

___ ___ ___ ___ ___ ___ ___ ___ ___
2   14 10 15 18 18 13 10 15

___ ___ ___ ___ ___ ___ !
7   13 2   4   15 2

Secret Code

4 = h	15 = e	13 = i	7 = d
2 = s	10 = t	12 = p	9 = n
8 = b	18 = l	11 = o	14 = a

Beginning at the star, cross out the first letter and every other letter in the grid. Then, write the remaining letters, in order, to solve the riddle.

★ m →	a	h	j
c →	u	z	n
l →	g	o	l
k →	e	t	g
h →	y	f	m

Where does a lion go to exercise?

___ ___ ___ ___ ___ ___

___ ___ ___ !

Choose a word from the word list to complete each sentence. Write the words in order from left to right along the chain, one letter in each circle. Then, write the numbered letters, in order, to solve the riddle.

1. Feed the horse _____.
2. Pete has a _____ train.
3. We had _____ and rice for dinner.
4. The autumn _____ was orange.
5. Can you _____ the flute?

Word List

beans   play
hay   toy
leaf

What do you get when you cross a bumblebee with a rabbit?

a ____ ____ ____ ____ ____ bunny!

Use the secret code to solve the riddle.

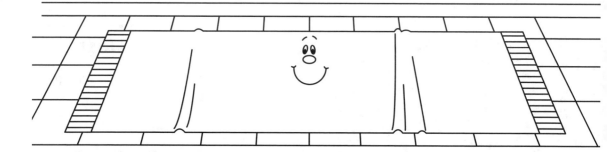

What did the rug say to the floor?

___ ___ ___ ___ ___   ___ ___ ___
9   2   7   3   5   10   4   6

___ ___ ___ ___ ___ ___ ___!
 8   4   3   5   0   5   1

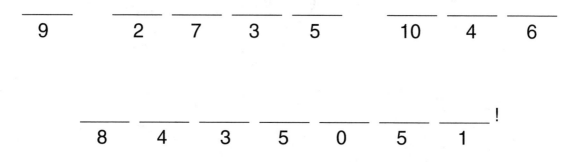

Secret Code

7 = a	11 = s	2 = h	6 = u
9 = I	15 = g	5 = e	1 = d
3 = v	18 = f	8 = c	10 = y
4 = o	16 = t	0 = r	13 = b

Write the correct vowel to finish each word. Use the clues to finish the crossword puzzle.

Across

4. k ____ te

6. r ____ pe

7. gl ____ be

9. n ____ ne

10. r ____ ke

Down

1. c ____ ke

2. fl ____ te

3. sk ____ te

5. t ____ re

8. b ____ ne

9

Circle the word that is shown only one time in each box. Write the circled words, in order, to solve the riddle.

Ball	At	Small
Tall	At	Ball
Tall	All	Small

over	out	these
the	these	out
over	that	that

fun	for	pans
for	fans	fun
can	pans	can

leave	laugh
laugh	little
little	laugh

Why does it get hot after a baseball game?

_____ _____ _____ _____!

Use the secret code to solve the riddle.

Why didn't anyone want to sleep next to the father dinosaur?

__ __ __ __ __ __ __
50 15 60 70 20 25 15

__ __   __ __ __   __
90 15   85 70 25   70

__ __ __ __ __ __ _ __ __ __ __ __ __ !
50 75 55 45 30 55 25 45 55 75 20 25

Secret Code			
55 = o	90 = h	30 = t	70 = a
45 = n	25 = s	60 = c	20 = u
50 = B	15 = e	85 = w	75 = r

Write the correct vacation word from the word list in each sentence.
Find and circle the words in the puzzle.

1. Pack your _____ for the trip.

2. We went skiing in the _____.

3. My family wants to _____ in the city.

4. Carol loves to swim at the _____.

5. Everyone gets to _____ and have fun.

6. My cousins travel to see us each _____.

7. Sue is going to Florida for a _____.

8. My brother likes to _____ to different places.

```
s  u  i  t  c  a  s  e  i  o
r  j  p  v  o  b  e  a  c  h
t  o  e  s  y  w  t  d  f  o
r  v  n  y  p  m  a  r  e  l
a  s  i  g  h  t  s  e  e  i
v  f  m  e  f  z  f  l  y  d
e  z  q  p  u  n  d  a  h  a
l  t  d  d  p  b  h  x  f  y
m  o  u  n  t  a  i  n  s  d
k  v  a  c  a  t  i  o  n  v
```

Word List

beach
holiday
mountains
relax
sightsee
suitcase
travel
vacation

Use the secret code to solve the riddle.

What kind of puzzle never sits still?

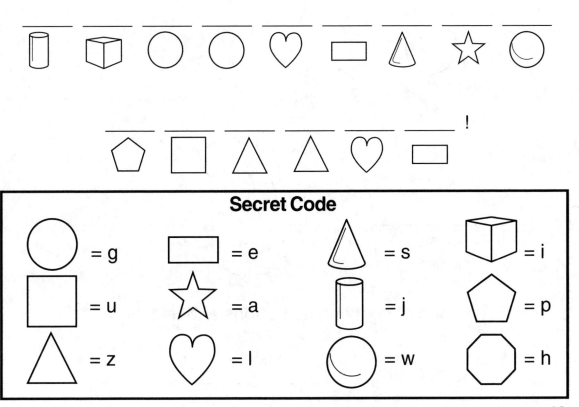

Choose a word from the word list to complete each sentence. Write the words in order from left to right along the chain, one letter in each circle. Then, write the numbered letters in order to solve the riddle.

1. Put the shells in the _____.
2. My dad rides the _____ to work.
3. The squirrel has a bushy _____.
4. Dave's bicycle _____ is broken.
5. Follow the _____ to the lake.

Word List

chain   train
pail   tail
trail

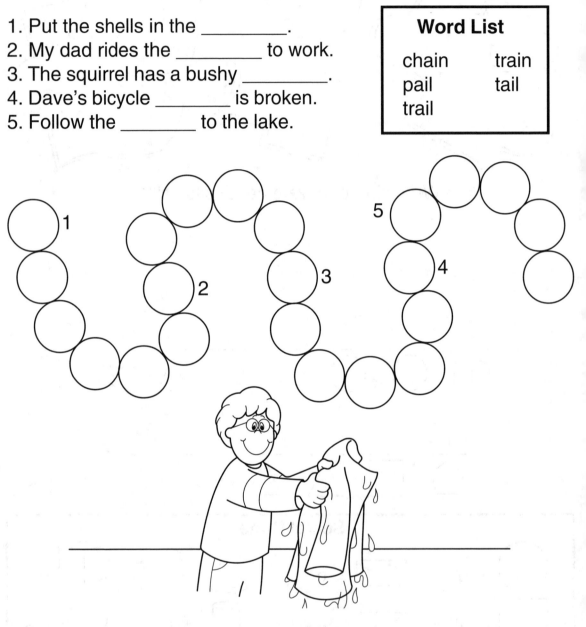

What kind of coat has no buttons and is put on wet?

a coat of ____ ____ ____ ____ ____ !

Beginning at the star, cross out the first letter and every other letter in the grid. Then, write the remaining letters, in order, to solve the riddle.

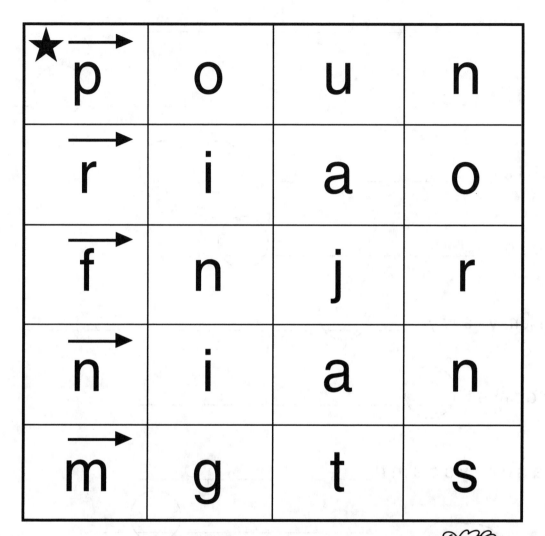

★→ p	o	u	n
→ r	i	a	o
→ f	n	j	r
→ n	i	a	n
→ m	g	t	s

What jewelry do vegetables wear?

___ ___ ___ ___ ___

___ ___ ___ ___ ___ !

Unscramble each space word and write it on the lines. Then, write the circled letters, in order, to solve the riddle.

xalgay __ __ ⬭ ⬭ __ __

asturnoat __ __ __ __ __ __ __ ⬭ __

chlaun __ __ __ ⬭ ⬭ ⬭

torbi __ __ __ __ ⬭

ilkmy awy __ ⬭ __ __ __ __ __ __

eormet ⬭ __ __ __ __ __

lasor yssemt __ __ __ __ __

__ __ __ __ ⬭ __

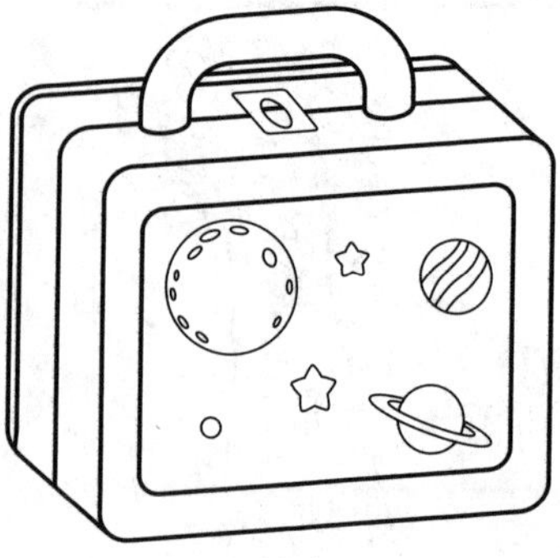

When does an astronaut eat?

at " __ __ __ __ __ __ __ __ __ __ __ "!

Write the correct word from the word list in each sentence. Use the clues to finish the crossword puzzle.

Across

2. Why is that girl _____?
4. The _____ was full of cookies.
6. My dad wants to _____ his car.
7. He saw the _____ in the pond.

Down

1. I ride the _____ to school.
3. Put the books on the _____.
4. The _____ was Sara's favorite toy.
5. The squirrel had a _____.

Word List

bus
desk
dish
doll
duck
nut
sad
sell

Write the correct camping word from the word list in each sentence.
Find and circle the words in the puzzle.

1. We went _____ through the forest.

2. I helped my dad put up the _____.

3. We told stories around the _____.

4. Use the _____ to see the bird.

5. Fill the _____ with cold water.

6. Let's roast _____ over the fire.

7. Tom went _____ on the rocks.

8. Paddle the _____ on the lake.

9. Put all the supplies in your _____.

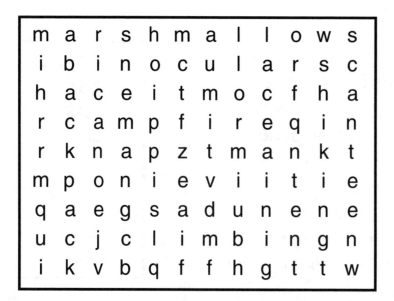

m	a	r	s	h	m	a	l	l	o	w	s
i	b	i	n	o	c	u	l	a	r	s	c
h	a	c	e	i	t	m	o	c	f	h	a
r	c	a	m	p	f	i	r	e	q	i	n
r	k	n	a	p	z	t	m	a	n	k	t
m	p	o	n	i	e	v	i	i	t	i	e
q	a	e	g	s	a	d	u	n	e	n	e
u	c	j	c	l	i	m	b	i	n	g	n
i	k	v	b	q	f	f	h	g	t	t	w

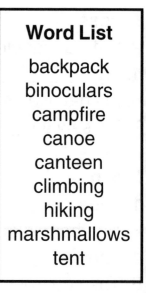

Word List

backpack
binoculars
campfire
canoe
canteen
climbing
hiking
marshmallows
tent

Use the secret code to solve the riddle.

Where do you leave your dog while you shop?

___ ___   ___ ___

___ ___ ___ ___ ___ ___ ___

___ ___ ___ !

Secret Code

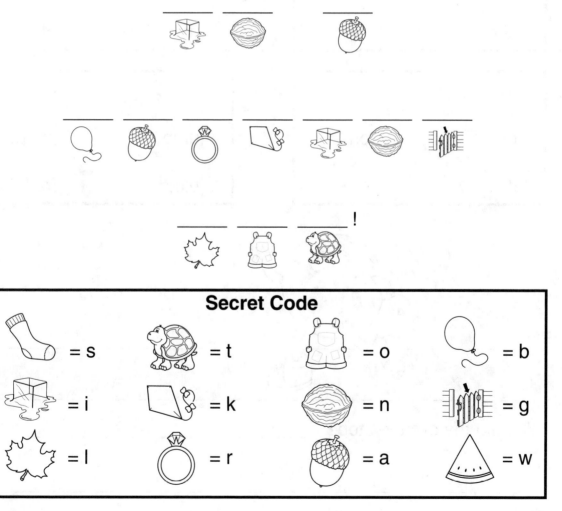

= s   = t   = o   = b

= i   = k   = n   = g

= l   = r   = a   = w

Circle the word that is shown only one time in each box. Write the circled words, in order, to solve the riddle below.

before	because
better	better
before	before

it	is
is	in
in	is

run	rug
rug	run
ran	rug

off	our
our	out
off	off

if	of
on	on
if	if

fruit	jump
jump	jump
juice	fruit

Why did the orange stop? _____ _____

_____ _____ _____ _____!

Unscramble each circus word and write it on the lines. Then, write the circled letters, in order, to solve the riddle.

l e n t e p h a   ___ ___ ___ ___ (___) ___ ___

n c l o w   (___) ___ ___ ___ ___

g h t t p e r o i   ___ ___ ___ ___ (___) ___ ___ ___

y m k o n e   ___ (___) ___ ___ ___ ___

g i b   p o t   (___) ___ ___   ___ ___ ___

c a r o b t a   ___ ___ ___ ___ ___ (___) ___

e e t r h   g i r n s   (___) ___ ___ ___ ___

___ ___ ___ ___ (___)

Which circus performers can see in the dark?

___ ___ ___ ___ ___ ___ ___ " ___ ___ " !

Choose the correct ending for each word and write it in the sentence. Use the completed words in the crossword puzzle.

Word Endings

ing   ed   s

Across

4. Tom yell_____, "Watch out!"

6. I jump_____ into the pool.

7. Jake was kick_____ the ball down the street.

9. He was shout_____ for his dog to fetch the ball.

10. The squirrel climb_____ the tree yesterday.

Down

1. Cindy walk_____ to school this morning.

2. Scott was talk_____ to his grandmother on the phone.

3. We were play_____ our last game of the year.

5. My brother run_____ three miles a day.

8. My sister ride_____ the bus to school.

Unscramble each animal word from the word list. Then, find and circle the words in the puzzle below.

gtorallia __ __ __ __ __ __ __ __ __

abzer __ __ __ __ __

taelphne __ __ __ __ __ __ __ __

aorongka __ __ __ __ __ __ __ __

lgorial __ __ __ __ __ __ __

ymoken __ __ __ __ __ __

gtire __ __ __ __ __

nlio __ __ __ __

igrafef __ __ __ __ __ __ __

e	l	e	p	h	a	n	t	b	e	a	f
x	r	m	p	z	z	l	r	c	w	g	m
z	z	w	e	w	l	t	x	g	i	o	g
r	e	a	l	l	i	g	a	t	o	r	i
x	b	k	o	s	o	l	q	i	b	i	r
v	r	h	k	l	n	v	u	g	g	l	a
s	a	i	e	n	u	y	c	e	t	l	f
o	x	p	x	j	z	t	l	r	i	a	f
m	o	n	k	e	y	f	e	c	l	w	e
k	a	n	g	a	r	o	o	x	s	u	g

Word List

alligator
elephant
giraffe
gorilla
kangaroo
lion
monkey
tiger
zebra

Choose a word from the word list to complete each sentence. Write the words in order from left to right along the chain, one letter in each circle. Then, write the numbered letters, in order, to solve the riddle.

1. Jamal let us swim in his _____.
2. You can _____ the pieces together.
3. Will scored the last _____.
4. We will have _____ for dessert.
5. My _____ is warm and cozy.
6. Set the table with forks and _____.

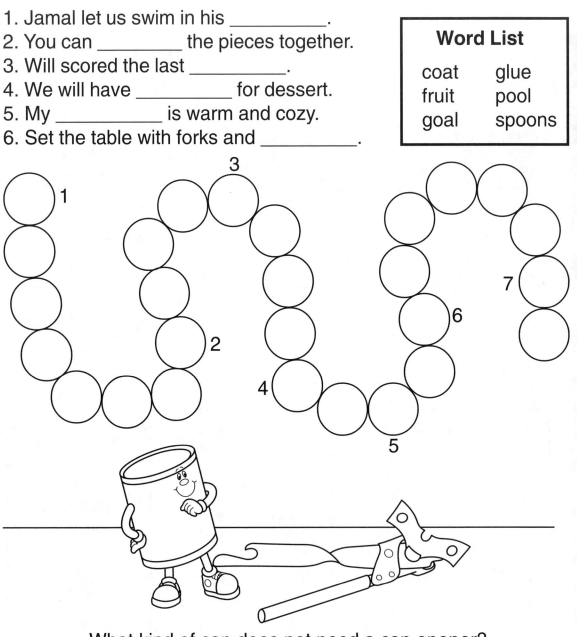

What kind of can does not need a can opener?

a ____ ____ ____ ____ ____ ____ ____ !

Use the secret code to solve the riddle.

What do birds use to clean their nests?

___ ___ ___ ___ ___ ___ ___
10 50 40 100 90 50 20

___ ___ ___ ___ ___ ___ ___ !
80 70 30 100 50 20 30

Secret Code			
30 = s	90 = h	20 = r	50 = e
10 = f	40 = a	70 = u	80 = d
60 = m	100 = t	0 = w	

Beginning at the star, cross out the first letter and every other letter in the grid. Then, write the letters, in order, to solve the riddle.

p	w	o	h	r	e	h	n
a	i	e	t	d	t	k	u
s	r	p	n	e	s	n	i
f	n	w	t	s	o	m	a
n	d	h	r	s	i	d	v
w	e	t	w	l	a	d	y

When is a car not a car?

___ ___ ___ ___   ___ ___   ___ ___ ___ ___ ___

___ ___ ___ ___   ___ ___

___ ___   ___ ___ ___ ___ ___ ___ ___ ___ !

Unscramble each bug word and write it on the lines. Then, write the circled letters in order to solve the riddle.

g o n d r f y l a ___ ___ ___ ___ ◯ ◯ ___ ___ ___

m w o r ◯ ◯ ___ ___ ___

r i c c k t e ___ ◯ ___ ___ ___ ___ ___

b l e b u b e e m ___ ___ ◯ ___ ___ ___ ___ ___ ___

d y b g a l u ___ ___ ◯ ___ ___ ___ ___

n a t ◯ ___ ___

u t t b f y r e l ___ ___ ___ ___ ___ ___ ___ ___ ◯ ___

p s d e r i ◯ ___ ___ ___ ___ ___

When do robins like to play outside?

___ ___ ___   " ___ ___ ___ ___ ___ "

___ ___ ___ ___ !

Unscramble each garden word from the word list. Then, find the words in the puzzle below.

l o s n f w r e u   __ __ __ __ __ __ __ __ __

y a i s d   __ __ __ __ __

r g d e n a   __ __ __ __ __ __

l w t o r e   __ __ __ __ __ __

d s p a e   __ __ __ __ __

p t u l i   __ __ __ __ __

e o h   __ __ __

k r a e   __ __ __ __

d l a f f o d i   __ __ __ __ __ __ __ __

f	x	b	a	u	h	s	g	t	d	u	a
s	u	n	f	l	o	w	e	r	a	o	h
n	v	y	i	z	e	h	n	o	f	z	l
x	d	r	m	f	m	m	w	w	f	g	w
g	a	r	d	e	n	q	e	e	o	j	b
l	i	q	z	m	l	v	j	l	d	h	r
q	s	r	h	z	n	y	p	v	i	w	a
t	y	y	t	u	l	i	p	m	l	e	k
l	r	m	v	v	w	j	s	p	a	d	e

Word List

daffodil
daisy
garden
hoe
rake
spade
sunflower
trowel
tulip

Write the correct word from the word list in each sentence. Use the clues to finish the crossword puzzle.

Across

2. Sue's _____ has tiny furniture inside.

4. He rode his _____ down the street.

6. Pam bounced the _____ down the court.

Down

1. The girls played _____ at recess.

3. Sam hit the _____ over the fence.

5. Carol pulled her little brother in a _____.

7. Our _____ flew high in the sky.

8. My new _____ has a basket and a horn.

Word List
baseball
basketball
bike
dollhouse
jump rope
kite
scooter
wagon

Circle the word that is shown only one time in each box. Write the circled words, in order, to solve the riddle below.

Do	Go	To
So	To	Go
To	To	So

yes	your	yet
your	two	yes
yet	two	you

knee	know	knew
keep	new	keep
knew	new	knee

and	any	all
also	also	all
all	and	also

shirt	stay	start
stay	short	snow
start	snow	shirt

can	color	caps
color	cats	cats
cuts	caps	can

What did one barber ask the other? _____ _____

_____ _____ _____-_____?

Word Puzzles and Games: Grade 2 Answer Key

Page 1   comet books!

Page 2   They both have bark!

Page 3

Across	Down
2. duck	1. ax
4. box	3. car
5. ring	4. bug
7. pot	6. net
8. egg	7. pig

Page 4
(Answers read from left to right.)

chocolate	sundae
pizza	popcorn
spaghetti	pancake
hamburger	a cupcake!

Page 5   on satellite dishes!

Page 6   a jungle gym!

Page 7

1. hay	2. toy
3. beans	4. leaf
5. play	a honey bunny!

Page 8   I have you covered!

Page 9

Across	Down
4. kite	1. cake
6. rope	2. flute
7. globe	3. skate
9. nine	5. tire
10. rake	8. bone

Page 10   All the fans leave!

Page 11
Because he was a Bronto-snorus!

Page 12

1. suitcase	2. mountains
3. sightsee	4. beach
5. relax	6. holiday
7. vacation	8. travel

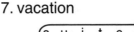

Page 13   a jigglesaw puzzle!

Page 14

1. pail	2. train
3. tail	4. chain
5. trail	a coat of paint!

Page 15   onion rings!

Page 16
(Answers read from left to right.)

galaxy	astronaut
launch	orbit
milky way	meteor
solar system	at "launch"time!

Page 17

Across	Down
2. sad	1. bus
4. dish	3. desk
6. sell	4. doll
7. duck	5. nut

A

Page 18

1. hiking
2. tent
3. campfire
4. binoculars
5. canteen
6. marshmallows
7. climbing
8. canoe
9. backpack

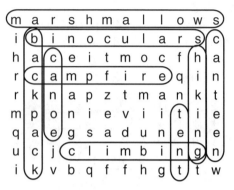

Page 19

in a barking lot!

Page 20

because it ran out of juice!

Page 21

(Answers read from left to right.)

elephant — clown
tightrope — monkey
big top — acrobat
three rings — acro"bats"

Page 22

Across
4. yelled
6. jumped
7. kicking
9. shouting
10. climbed

Down
1. walked
2. talking
3. playing
5. runs
8. rides

Page 23

(Answers read from left to right.)

alligator — zebra
elephant — kangaroo
gorilla — monkey
tiger — lion
giraffe

Page 23 continued

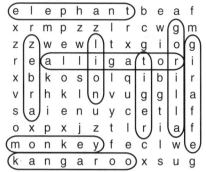

Page 24

1. pool
2. glue
3. goal
4. fruit
5. coat
6. spoons
a pelican!

Page 25

feather dusters!

Page 26

when it turns into a driveway!

Page 27

(Answers read from left to right.)

dragonfly — worm
cricket — bumblebee
ladybug — ant
butterfly — spider
on "worm" days!

Page 28

(Answers read from left to right.)

sunflower — daisy
garden — trowel
spade — tulip
hoe — rake
daffodil

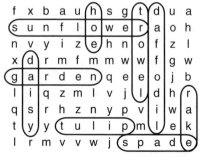

B

Page 29

Across
2. dollhouse
4. scooter
6. basketball

Down
1. jump rope
3. baseball
5. wagon
7. kite
8. bike

Page 30   Do you know any short-cuts?

Page 31   in a "hen"velope!

Page 32
1. paint
3. feet
5. mail
its tail!

2. seeds
4. cream
6. peel

Page 33   the catcher and the umpire!

Page 34
(Answers are read from left to right.)

eagle
owl
snake
woodchuck
frog

squirrel
opossum
deer
raccoon
a groundhog!

Page 35

Across
1. neck
3. pocket
6. king
8. dress
9. lamp

Down
2. clock
3. pants
4. kitten
5. turtle
7. jump

Page 36
because the class was so bright!

Page 37   a mouse going on vacation!

Page 38
(Answers are read from left to right.)

tundra
ocean
glacier
"late for dinner!"

Arctic fox
narwhal
polar bear

© Carson-Dellosa CD-4538

Page 39   a "sty"-scraper!

Page 40

elephant — gosling — penguin
hatchling — shark — chick
turtle — calf — goose
pup — frog ——— tadpole

```
p  o  o  d (s  h  a  r  k) t
(e  l  e  p  h  a  n  t) p  a
d  i (t  u  r  t  l  e) f  d
(g  y  q  w  i  c  o  d  y  p
o  b  y  i (c  h  i  c  k) o
s  f  m  a  y  l  s  a  s  l
l  r  w  t  d  i  c  l  z  e
i  o  b  x  p  n (p) f  g  u
n  g (p  e  n  g  u  i  n) p
(g  o  o  s  e) u  p  q  l  p
```

Page 41

Across
3. white
5. note
7. joke
8. tube
9. snake

Down
1. rule
2. time
3. wrote
4. eve
6. these

Page 42
He wanted to have sweet dreams!

Page 43   a flea market!

Page 44
1. bee
3. suit
5. juice
7. gray

2. wheel
4. blue
6. May
a blue jay!

Page 45
(Answers read from left to right.)

kick ball
soccer
gymnastics
softball
baseball
(puzzle solution on page D)

dodgeball
track
football
basketball

C

Page 45 continued

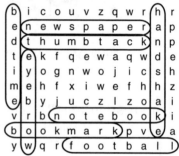

Page 46

Across
3. teacher
5. dirt
6. corn
7. yard
8. farm

Down
1. bird
2. shark
3. turn
4. store
6. card

Page 47   a spelling bee!

Page 48   Where on earth have you been?

Page 49

Across
1. arm
2. horses
4. turtle
6. horn

Down
1. after
2. herd
3. shirt
5. turn
6. hammer
7. nurse

Page 50

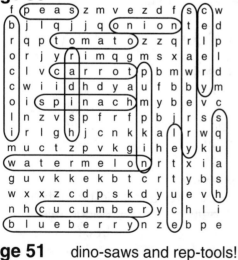

Page 51   dino-saws and rep-tools!

Page 52   nothing, it just waved!
D

Page 53

Across
2. powder
6. boiled
7. about
9. house

Down
1. town
2. point
3. enjoy
4. flower
5. cow
8. boy

Page 54   It has the most stories!

Page 55

Lines should be drawn to make the following words: newspaper, thumbtack, handshake, bedtime, eyebrow, football, bookmark, and notebook.

```
b i c o u v z q w r h r
e n e w s p a p e r a p
d t h u m b t a c k n p
t e k f q e w a q w d e
i y o g n w o j i c s h
m e h f x i w e f h h z
e b y j u c z l z o a i
v r b n o t e b o o k i
b o o k m a r k p v e a
y w q r f o o t b a l l
```

Page 56

because they brush with honey combs!

Page 57   because it was a"head"!

Page 58   I have a lot of problems!

Page 59

Lines should be drawn to make the following words: sunflower, chalkboard, spaceship, toothbrush, homework, firefly, goldfish, and horseshoe.

```
h t t o o t h b r u s h
o v f x g q j t s n u g
m c k e y w y u n v n o
e s p a c e s h i p f l
w b p k y v a n i e l d
o p n e z u f j p o o f
r g y f n z m v t q w i
k f i r e f l y c v e s
h o r s e s h o e k r h
c h a l k b o a r d m i
```

Page 60   He wanted to tie the game!

Beginning at the star, cross out the first letter and every other letter in the grid. Then, write the remaining letters, in order, to solve the riddle.

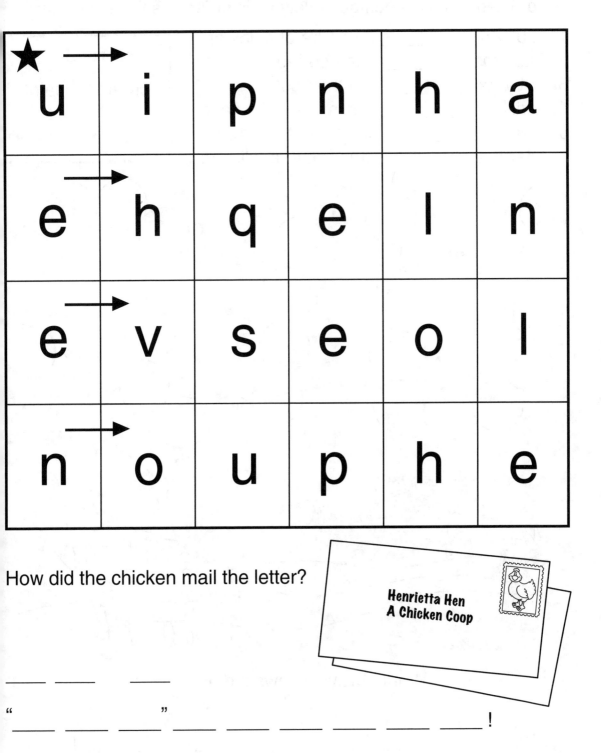

How did the chicken mail the letter?

Henrietta Hen
A Chicken Coop

___ __ ____

" _____ "

___ __ ___ _____ _____ ____ !

Choose a word from the word list to complete each sentence. Write the words in order from left to right along the chain, one letter in each circle. Then, write the numbered letters, in order, to solve the riddle.

1. You can _____ a picture of a flower.
2. Plant the _____ in the spring.
3. Put your _____ on the floor.
4. Vanilla ice _____ is my favorite flavor.
5. Please _____ the letter tomorrow.
6. After you _____ the banana, slice it.

<table>
<tr><th colspan="2">Word List</th></tr>
<tr><td>cream</td><td>paint</td></tr>
<tr><td>feet</td><td>peel</td></tr>
<tr><td>mail</td><td>seeds</td></tr>
</table>

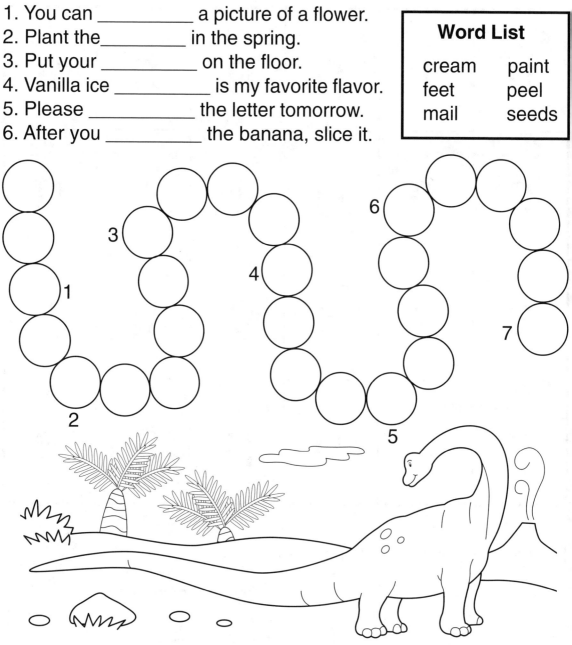

What always follows a dinosaur?

____ ____ ____   ____ ____ ____ ____!

Beginning at the star, cross out the first letter and every other letter in the grid. Then, write the remaining letters, in order, to solve the riddle.

★→							
s	c	p	a	f	t	h	c
y	h	o	e	d	r	q	a
x	n	k	d	i	t	r	h
s	e	m	u	f	m	n	p
j	i	b	r	l	e	a	!

You leave home and take three left turns. When you get home there are two people in masks. Who are they?

the ___ ___ ___ ___ ___ ___ ___   ___ ___ ___

___ ___ ___   ___ ___ ___ ___ ___ ___ ___ ___

Unscramble each animal name and write it on the lines. Then, write the circled letters, in order, to solve the riddle.

g l e a e   ___ ___ (___) ___ ___

l q s u r r i e   ___ ___ ___ ___ ___ (___) ___ ___

l o w   (___) ___ ___

m p s o o s u   ___ ___ ___ ___ ___ (___) ___

k s a n e   ___ (___) ___ ___ ___

e r d e   (___) ___ ___ ___

d o o w h u c c k   ___ ___ ___ ___ ___ (___) ___ ___ ___

c n o o c r a   ___ ___ ___ ___ (___) ___ ___

f g o r   ___ ___ ___ (___)

What do you get when you cross a pig and a pile of dirt?

a   ___ ___ ___ ___ ___ ___ ___ ___ ___!

Write the correct word from the word list in each sentence. Use the clues to finish the crossword puzzle.

Across

1. Sara wore a scarf around her _____.
3. Put the coins in your _____.
6. The _____ wore a gold crown.
8. My new _____ is pink and white.
9. Turn off the _____ when you leave.

Down

2. The _____ reads 2:30.
3. Tom wore blue _____ and brown shoes.
4. The _____ was brown and black.
5. The _____ is on the log.
7. Tim had to _____ over the puddle.

Word List

clock
dress
jump
king
kitten
lamp
neck
pants
pocket
turtle

Circle the word that is shown only one time in each box. Write the circled words, in order, to solve the riddle below.

cause	bear	bear
brush	because	brush
bear	brush	cause

than	those	there
those	the	than
than	there	those

glass	class	pass
club	pass	club
pass	club	glass

were	was	wish
were	wish	want
want	way	way

go	to	no
no	to	no
so	to	go

might	light	right
light	flight	bright
flight	might	right

Why did the teacher wear sunglasses? _____ _____

_____ _____ _____ _____ !

Use the secret code to solve the riddle.

What is gray, has four legs, and a trunk?

___   ___ ___ ___ ___ ___
74   36   45   42   92   77

___ ___ ___ ___ ___   ___ ___
21   45   39   46   21   45   46

___ ___ ___ ___ ___ ___ ___ ___ !
82   74   56   74   89   39   45   46

Secret Code			
45 = o	36 = m	77 = e	56 = c
21 = g	46 = n	89 = t	92 = s
82 = v	74 = a	42 = u	39 = i

Unscramble each polar word and write it on the lines. Then, write the circled letters, in order, to solve the riddle.

d a r n t u   ___ ___ ___ (___) ___ ___

r c i c A t   x f o   ___ ___ ___ ___ (___) ___
                      ___ ___ ___ ___

n o c e a   ___ ___ ___ (___)

r a n l h a w   (___) ___ ___ ___ ___ ___ ___

l i e g a c r   ___ ___ ___ ___ (___) ___

r a p o l   r e a b   ___ ___ ___ ___ ___
                      ___ ___ ___ (___)

What should you never call a penguin?

"late for ___ ___ ___ ___ ___ ___!"

Color the blocks that have nouns. Then, write the remaining letters, in order, to solve the riddle.

m table	a jump	s pretty	t walk
y slow	s small	c talk	d cat
r nice	a skip	p give	d tree
r mom	e run	a baby	t school
r blue	o bed	g house	d ring

What do you call an 800-foot pig pen?

____ " ____ ____ ____ - ____ ____ ____ ____ ____ ____ ____ " !

Draw a line to match each animal name to the correct animal baby name. Then, find and circle all of the words in the puzzle below.

elephant	gosling	penguin
hatchling	shark	chick
turtle	calf	goose
pup	frog	tadpole

```
p o o d s h a r k t
e l e p h a n t p a
d i t u r t l e f d
g y q w i c o d y p
o b y i c h i c k o
s f m a y l s a s l
l r w t d i c l z e
i o b x p n p f g u
n g p e n g u i n p
g o o s e u p q l p
```

Write the correct word from the word list in each sentence. Use the clues to finish the crossword puzzle.

Across

3. The coat was red and _____.

5. Leave a _____ for Mom and Dad.

7. Dan told a funny _____.

8. Squeeze the _____ of toothpaste.

9. There was a _____ in the garden.

Down

1. Mrs. Smith has a _____ about chewing gum.

2. Do we have _____ to visit Sandra?

3. Tamika _____ a report on China.

4. It was the _____ of her birthday party.

6. Put _____ bags on the table.

Word List

eve
joke
note
rule
these
time
tube
snake
white
wrote

Circle the word that is shown only one time in each box. Write the circled words, in order, to solve the riddle below.

She	He	Me
Be	She	Be
Me	Be	She

would	watch	while
while	wanted	water
water	watch	would

too	the	two
the	too	to
two	too	too

has	has	here
how	here	how
how	have	has

swim	sweet	swam
swim	sweat	swim
swam	swam	sweat

dreams	drink	draw
teams	draw	teams
leaf	drink	leaf

Why did the boy put sugar on his pillow? _____ _____

_____ _____ _____ _____!

Color the blocks that have verbs. Then, write the remaining letters, in order, to solve the riddle.

o swim	a dog	w cry	f pan
l pizza	f write	e sister	a fish
z eat	m pencil	a tired	r look
r nice	k door	e tall	d find
g ride	t laugh	t red	y walk

What kind of market does a dog hate?

___ ___ ___ ___ ___

___ ___ ___ ___ ___ ___ !

Choose a word from the word list to complete each sentence. Write the words in order from left to right along the chain, one letter in each circle. Then, write the numbered letters, in order, to solve the riddle.

1. The _____ landed on the flower.
2. A unicycle has only one _____.
3. I wore a bathing _____ to the beach.
4. The jeans were _____.
5. We had cereal and orange _____.
6. Her birthday is in _____.
7. The sky was rainy and _____.

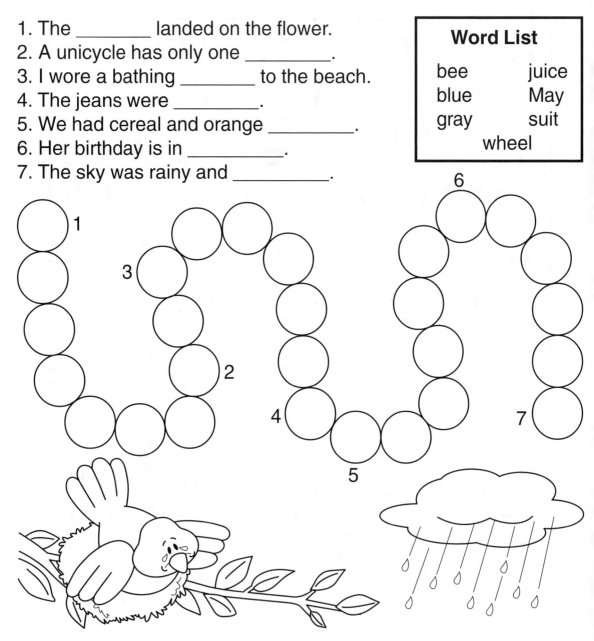

Word List

bee	juice
blue	May
gray	suit
	wheel

What bird is always sad?

a ____ ____ ____ ____ ____ ____ ____ !

44

Unscramble each sports word from the word list. Then, find and circle the words in the puzzle below.

k k i c   l b l a   __ __ __ __   __ __ __ __

b l l a d d o g e   __ __ __ __ __ __ __ __ __

r c c s o e   __ __ __ __ __ __

c t r a k   __ __ __ __ __

m c s t y g n a i s   __ __ __ __ __ __ __ __ __ __

t o o b f a l l   __ __ __ __ __ __ __ __

f s b a l o t l   __ __ __ __ __ __ __ __

a b b a l s k e t l   __ __ __ __ __ __ __ __ __ __

b l l b a s e a   __ __ __ __ __ __ __ __

d	o	d	g	e	b	a	l	l	d	a	x
k	k	u	y	u	a	c	q	z	i	b	f
i	k	s	m	j	s	o	c	c	e	r	o
c	k	o	n	b	k	h	t	z	r	n	o
k	d	f	a	x	e	q	g	a	t	i	t
b	a	t	s	k	t	r	a	c	k	w	b
a	x	b	t	c	b	y	w	o	e	f	a
l	z	a	i	b	a	s	e	b	a	l	l
l	j	l	c	s	l	w	b	d	p	a	l
m	e	l	s	n	l	j	g	c	d	x	s

Word List

baseball
basketball
dodgeball
football
gymnastics
kick ball
soccer
softball
track

Write the correct word from the word list in each sentence. Use the clues to finish the crossword puzzle.

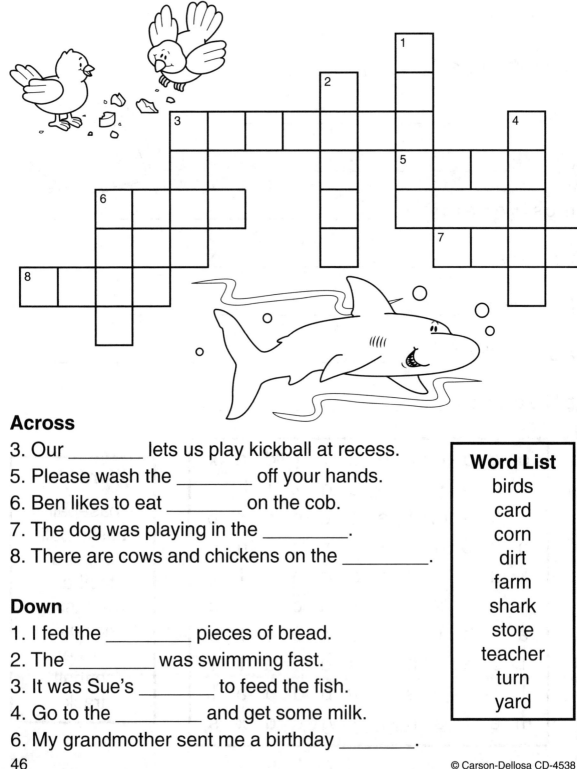

Across

3. Our _____ lets us play kickball at recess.
5. Please wash the _____ off your hands.
6. Ben likes to eat _____ on the cob.
7. The dog was playing in the _____.
8. There are cows and chickens on the _____.

Down

1. I fed the _____ pieces of bread.
2. The _____ was swimming fast.
3. It was Sue's _____ to feed the fish.
4. Go to the _____ and get some milk.
6. My grandmother sent me a birthday _____.

Word List
birds
card
corn
dirt
farm
shark
store
teacher
turn
yard

46

Color the blocks that have adjectives. Then, write the remaining letters, in order, to solve the riddle.

t green	a boy	s play	p car
n happy	e dad	l bird	k funny
l grass	i rock	s tiny	n drink
g hop	r soft	b pen	g short
b cloudy	e cloud	e water	d loud

What animal is smarter than a talking parrot?

___ ____ ___ __ ____ ___ ___

__ ___ ___ !

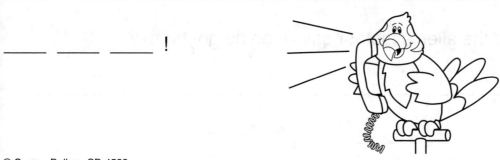

Circle the word that is shown only one time in each box. Write the circled words, in order, to solve the riddle below.

Where	When	Why
Why	Who	Who
Who	When	Why

of	on	to
to	in	of
off	off	in

eat	eight	each
each	earth	each
eight	eat	eat

how	here	him
had	him	had
here	how	have

yet	yes	you
your	yet	yellow
yes	yellow	your

been	be	before
best	bell	best
before	bell	be

What did the alien's mother say when he got home?

_____   _____   _____   _____

_____   _____ ?

Write the correct word from the word list in each sentence. Use the clues to finish the crossword puzzle.

Across

1. I have a scratch on my _____.
2. I like to ride _____.
4. The _____ crawled in his shell.
6. The _____ made a loud sound.

Down

1. Carla went to the park _____ school.
2. The _____ of sheep were eating grass.
3. My new _____ is blue and white.
5. Please _____ on the hot water.
6. Use a _____ to pound the nail into the wall.
7. The _____ took my temperature.

Word List
after
arm
hammer
herd
horn
horses
nurse
shirt
turn
turtle

Find and circle each fruit or vegetable name in the puzzle below.

blueberry	lettuce	spinach
broccoli	onion	squash
carrot	peas	strawberry
celery	pumpkin	tomato
cucumber	radish	watermelon

```
f p e a s z m v e z d f s c w
b j l q j j q o n i o n t e d
r q p t o m a t o z z q r l p
o r j y r i m q g m s x a e l
c l v c a r r o t p b m w r d
c w i i d h d y a u f b b y m
o i s p i n a c h m y b e v c
l n z v s p f r f p b j r s s
i r l g h j c n k k a l r w q
m u c t z p v k g i h e y k u
w a t e r m e l o n r t x i a
g u v k k e k b t c r t y b s
w x x z c d p s k d y u e v h
n h c u c u m b e r y c h l i
b l u e b e r r y n z e b p e
```

Use the secret code to solve the riddle.

What did dinosaurs use to fix their homes?

d i n o - s a w s

a n d

r e p - t o o l s !

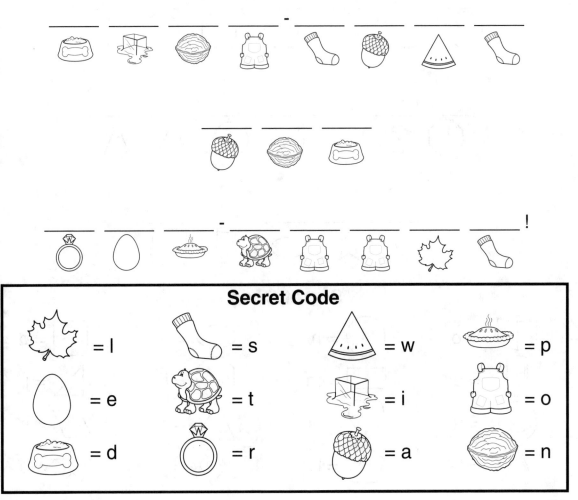

Secret Code

🍁 = l   🧦 = s   🍉 = w   🥧 = p

🥚 = e   🐢 = t   (ice) = i   (overalls) = o

(dog bowl) = d   💍 = r   (acorn) = a   (walnut) = n

Use the secret code to solve the riddle.

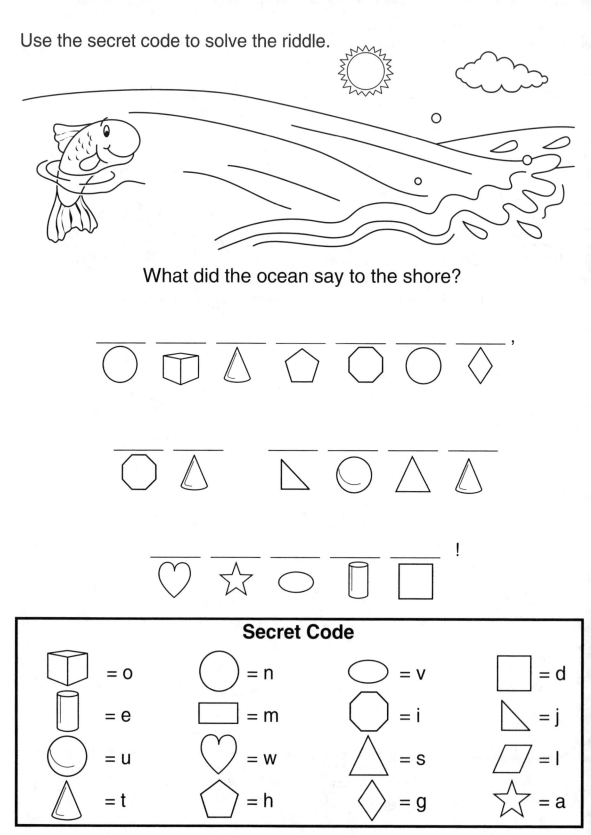

What did the ocean say to the shore?

___ ___ ___ ___ ___ ___ ___ ,
○ ▢ △ ⬠ ⬡ ○ ◇

___ ___   ___ ___ ___ ___
⬡ △   ◺ ◔ △ △

___ ___ ___ ___ ___ !
♡ ☆ ⬭ ▯ ▢

Secret Code

cube = o	circle = n	oval = v	square = d
cylinder = e	rectangle = m	octagon = i	triangle(right) = j
sphere = u	heart = w	triangle = s	parallelogram = l
cone = t	pentagon = h	diamond = g	star = a

Write the correct word from the word list in each sentence. Use the clues to finish the crossword puzzle.

Across

2. Put the _____ in the baby's bag.

6. Mom _____ water to make tea.

7. This book is _____ a pig and a spider.

9. Candice came to my _____ to visit.

Down

1. My _____ has a great baseball team.

2. Please _____ to the right answer on the board.

3. I really _____ reading books.

4. The _____ garden was in full bloom.

5. The _____ is sleeping in the barn.

8. That _____ rides his bike to school.

Word List

about
boiled
boy
cow
enjoy
flower
house
point
powder
town

Circle the word that is shown only one time in each box. Write the circled words, in order, to solve the riddle below.

Is	It	In
On	In	On
On	Is	Is

his	had	him
had	has	her
him	her	his

he	we	he
them	the	that
we	that	them

must	much	just
my	my	much
most	just	must

store	story	store
stories	stove	story
stove	stove	story

LIBRARY

Why is the library the tallest building in town? _____

_____ _____ _____ _____!

Draw a line to match one word from each column to make a compound word. Then, find and circle the compound words in the puzzle.

SUN   SHINE

news	tack
thumb	mark
hand	time
bed	book
eye	paper
foot	shake
book	ball
note	brow

```
b  i  c  o  u  v  z  q  w  r  h  r
e  n  e  w  s  p  a  p  e  r  a  p
d  t  h  u  m  b  t  a  c  k  n  p
t  e  k  f  q  e  w  a  q  w  d  e
i  y  o  g  n  w  o  j  i  c  s  h
m  e  h  f  x  i  w  e  f  h  h  z
e  b  y  j  u  c  z  l  z  o  a  i
v  r  b  n  o  t  e  b  o  o  k  i
b  o  o  k  m  a  r  k  p  v  e  a
y  w  q  r  f  o  o  t  b  a  l  l
```

Circle the word that is shown only one time in each box. Write the circled words, in order, to answer the riddle below.

between	behind
because	behind
behind	between

the	them	their
their	they	that
that	them	the

bird	brown	book
bring	bring	brush
brown	book	bird

will	wish	will
wish	while	wish
while	with	will

money	high	honey
home	high	home
home	money	high

come	combs	cone
cone	cob	cone
cob	cob	come

Why do bees have sticky hair? _____ _____

_____ _____ _____ _____!

Use the secret code to solve the riddle.

Why did the cabbage win the race?

$\overline{}$ $\overline{}$ $\overline{}$ $\overline{}$ $\overline{}$ $\overline{}$ $\overline{}$
600 500 100 900 200 400 500

$\overline{}$ $\overline{}$ $\overline{}$ $\overline{}$ $\overline{}$
300 800   999 900 400

          "
$\overline{}$ $\overline{}$ $\overline{}$ $\overline{}$ $\overline{}$ " !
900 700 500 900 1,000

Secret Code			
200 = u	700 = h	800 = t	400 = s
900 = a	100 = c	300 = i	999 = w
500 = e	600 = b	1, 000 = d	

Circle the word that is shown only one time in each box. Write the circled words, in order, to solve the riddle below.

A	My	A
My	I	We
A	We	My

him	him	has
hat	have	ham
has	ham	hat

at	a	as
as	an	am
an	am	at

lit	lot	look
like	look	like
love	love	lit

if	off	if
for	four	of
off	four	for

please		program
problems		please
program		please

$$2 \quad 1 \quad 4 \quad 5$$
$$\underline{+2} \quad \underline{+2} \quad \underline{+3} \quad \underline{+4}$$
$$4 \quad 3 \quad 7 \quad 9$$

$1 - 0 = 1$ $4 - 3 = 1$
$7 - 5 = 2$ $6 - 4 = 2$
$8 - 3 = 5$

What did one math book say to the other?_____ _____

_____ _____ _____ _____ !

58

© Carson-Dellosa CD-4538© Carson-Dellosa CD-4538

Draw a line to match one word from each column to make a compound word. Then, find and circle the compound words in the puzzle below.

CUP

CAKE

sun	ship
chalk	brush
space	fly
tooth	flower
home	shoe
fire	work
gold	fish
horse	board

```
h  t  t  o  o  t  h  b  r  u  s  h
o  v  f  x  g  q  j  t  s  n  u  g
m  c  k  e  y  w  y  u  n  v  n  o
e  s  p  a  c  e  s  h  i  p  f  l
w  b  p  k  y  v  a  n  i  e  l  d
o  p  n  e  z  u  f  j  p  o  o  f
r  g  y  f  n  z  m  v  t  q  w  i
k  f  i  r  e  f  l  y  c  v  e  s
h  o  r  s  e  s  h  o  e  k  r  h
c  h  a  l  k  b  o  a  r  d  m  i
```

Circle the word that is shown only one time in each box. Write the circled words, in order, to solve the riddle below.

Me	He	Me
Be	My	By
By	My	Be

will	were	what
wanted	where	what
were	where	will

to	the	two
the	tell	take
two	take	tell

try	fry	try
why	pie	why
pie	tie	fry

he	we	three
be	three	he
we	the	be

same	give	name
give	game	girl
name	girl	same

Why did the ball player bring a rope to the game?

_____ _____ _____ _____

_____ _____ !